THE COLLISION

Vol. 2

A Year of Cultural Conversations & Spiritual Collisions

Edited by Daniel Blackaby

THE COLLISION VOLUME TWO
A Year of Cultural Conversations & Spiritual Collisions

Published by Blackaby Minitries International
           P.O Box 1035
           Jonesboro, GA 30237
           Blackaby.org

Printed in the United States of America

Copyrighted © 2021 by Daniel Blackaby.

2021–1st ed

Cover design, interior design and typeset: Joni Le

ISBN 978-1-7350872-4-5

THE COLLISION

Equipping Christians to navigate today's digital, media-driven culture by strengthening their biblical foundations, addressing difficult questions about their faith, and guiding them to engage thoughtfully with today's pop culture and secular worldviews.

Table of Contents

Part Three: MOVIE REVIEWS

Introduction

Daniel Blackaby

Hello and welcome to The Collision!

If you are reading this book, then you have successfully navigated through the tempestuous year of 2020. Give yourself a pat on the back. You deserve it! What a crazy year it was. It had the unpredictability of an early M. Night Shaymalan film, the gritty tone of a David Fincher flick, and the unrelentingly violent onslaught of a Quentin Tarantino movie. I suspect that few tears were shed to see this chapter—at long last—disappear into the rearview mirror.

While 2020 was a difficult year for many individuals, it was a crucial year on a cultural level. It was punctuated by monumental cultural movements and seismic changes in the arts and entertainment industries. In short, it was a year filled with important cultural conversations in which Christians had much to learn and plenty of value to contribute.

In John 17 when Jesus commissioned His followers to be radically set apart from the surrounding culture but also actively present *in* that world, He did not attach any qualifiers or opt-out clauses. Circumstances change—pandemics hit, elections happen, worldviews clash in violent and distressing ways—but the Christian calling remains the same. Representing Christ as spiritually alive beings in a spiritually dead and increasingly anti-Christian world means collisions are inevitable. The question is how Christians navigate these collisions.

What to Expect?

This book is a snapshot. The articles selected for this annual volume were originally published on thecollision.org. Each of the amazing contributors loves Jesus and pop culture, and this book represents a year of how we collectively strove to collide with the world for Christ. Keep in mind that many of the world circumstances—the "collisions"—that led to the 20 articles in this volume are tied to a specific moment in time. For example, consider the following:

The forced closure of theaters around the world in 2020 put the movie industry into a prolonged hiatus. In the absence of new releases was a rise in popularity of retrospective and classic films. You'll find several nostalgic reviews in this book.

The nationwide lockdowns that ravaged many other sectors resulted in booming, record-breaking sales for the video game industry. How should Christians respond to the rapid influx of new gamers? You'll find some answers and guidelines here.

During a year of heightened outrage and discord, hashtag movements such as *#SilenceIsViolence* and *#CancelCulture* became widespread cultural talking points. A biblically based response to these movements is explored in this book.

At the same time, while the unique collisions of 2020 led to these articles, the foundational principals and approaches demonstrated throughout will, we hope, be applicable on a more general level. As I wrote in the introduction to *The Collision: Vol. 1*, this book is not just about collisions; it's about *colliders* and what it looks like to become one.

About the Collision

Some of you have been on the crazy little Collision train since the beginning and will be placing this book alongside last year's *Vol. 1* on your bookshelf. Know that we deeply appreciate your continual support. Others of you may have never heard of The Collision and were given this book as a gift from friends or family (you are clearly blessed with some wonderful people in your life!). Perhaps some of you stumbled across this book in a store or online and bought it on a whim.

The Collision was launched as a digital, multimedia platform aimed at equipping Christians to navigate the inevitable collisions between Christ and culture. By leveraging online articles, YouTube videos, books, podcasts, livestreams, and social media, we seek to cultivate honest cultural conversations about the important issues Christians face today.

I hope you will consider joining our community of culturally engaged Christians from around the world as together we collide with the world for Christ. Join the movement by connecting with us.

Website: thecollision.org
YouTube: youtube.com/c/thecollisionbmi
Facebook: @thecollisionbmi
Twitter: @thecollisionbmi

Part One

POP CULTURE COLLISIONS

1
How Should Christians Watch Movies?

Daniel Blackaby

There is a deeply rooted stigma in the Church against the movie and entertainment industry. Some Christians speak of "Hollywood" as the ominous equivalent to Mordor in Tolkien's *Lord of the Rings*. Despite this distrust, statistically speaking, Christians watch movies with the same frequency as non-Christians.

When it comes to cinema, Christians generally focus more on *what* than on *how*. They ask, "What movies are appropriate?" They give less attention to how to watch movies. Both issues are important. Today's Christians may watch movies at the same rate as non-Christians, but they shouldn't watch them the same way. When Jesus sent His followers into the world, He told them to be ***"wise as serpents and innocent as doves" (Matt. 10:16)***. Building upon that framework, here are five practical steps for how Christians should watch movies.

1. Enjoy Them

This might seem like an odd starting place. In fact, this aspect of the viewing experience is typically left out of Christian discussion altogether. Yet, at their base level, movies are entertainment. They can do far *more* than entertain—they can wrestle with deep philosophical and ethical themes and provide insightful social commentary—but these additional functions don't mean they can't also be enjoyed. Christians do not need to feel guilty about relishing a great film.

> Today's Christians may watch movies at the same rate as non-Christians, but they shouldn't watch them the same way.

2. Prepare

Christians should avoid going into a film blind. The looming threat of spoilers means you may need to tread carefully, but a general awareness of a movie's content is necessary.

This preliminary inquiry may save you from wasting money on a lousy movie. More importantly, it can alert you to any major causes of concern (a gratuitous sex scene, hard profanity, a militantly blasphemous tone, etc.) and allow you to take the necessary steps to protect your "dove-like" Christian innocence (for example, by waiting to watch the film at home so you can skip an unwholesome scene, watching it with an accountability partner, or avoiding it altogether).

3. Watch and Engage

People typically watch movies in order to shut their brains off and relax. But Christians should engage their mind while they watch. Finding a balance between enjoyment and engagement can be tricky, and actively engaging with the film runs the risk of reducing the experience to an intellectual exercise that strips cinema of its prime purpose.

But thoughtful engagement doesn't mean watching with a pen and paper in hand as you look for deep worldview implications in every camera pan or throwaway line of dialogue. It simply means being mentally present. When you watch a movie, you are entering into the world of the filmmaker. But you can—and *should*—remain in control of the experience.

4. Process and Review

Usually, our minds have already moved on to a dozen other thoughts by the time we return home from the theater, but one of the most important steps in the viewing experience comes immediately *after* watching a film. Intentionally take time to process what you've just seen. Push beyond the surface level of the plot or "it was good/bad." What worldview was presented? What insights about life did the movie provide? Do these insights line up with what the Bible teaches? If not, do they give you a better understanding of the opposing worldview?

5. Talk About It

Lastly, talk to other people about the movie. Watch it with a friend and then go grab coffee and discuss it afterward. Of course, you can also join the discussion digitally. Most people read movie reviews *before* watching a film (to determine whether to see it), but reading reviews and commentary *after* viewing a film is equally beneficial. Just because you didn't pick up on certain themes or attitudes the film presented doesn't mean they won't affect you. Allow other viewers to help you process what you may have missed.

Don't limit yourself to people who share your worldview or opinion. As a Christian, I appreciate hearing what other Christians are saying. But I also find it insightful to hear a secular perspective. If a film presents an anti-biblical worldview that turns me off, knowing why some unbelievers find that message inspiring helps me better understand the opposing worldview (even if I don't agree with).

2
Should Christians Play Video Games?

Daniel Blackaby

A Booming Industry

Despite often being excluded from the pantheon of cinema, music, and television, gaming has exploded into perhaps the most lucrative sector of the entertainment industry. While people typically think of cinema as the crown jewel of entertainment, the total worldwide box office in 2019 was a record $42.5 billion. That same year, the gaming industry hit a whopping $124.8 billion.

One study revealed that nearly 70% of Americans play video games. While the culturally ingrained image of a "gamer" is that of a pubescent boy sitting in his parents' basement playing an MMORPG (massive multiplayer online role-playing game), this stereotype has long been outdated. As many as 90% of video games are played on phones and tablets.

Also, while the 18–35 demographic contains the most frequent gamers, video games—driven largely by the shift from traditional consoles to mobile devices—are no longer the exclusive pastime of the young. People age 50+ are responsible for roughly 21% of gaming (the same percentage as gamers under 18). The less scientific "eyeball test" confirms this finding. While suit-wearing professionals once pored over spreadsheets and presentations on airplanes, mobile games are now their go-to inflight entertainment.

How Do Video Games Impact Society?

Video games carry a pointedly negative stigma, partially due to their relative newness in comparison to other entertainment mediums.

Another reason for their bad rap is that they most often become a topic of national conversation when taking the blame for horrific violent deeds. For example, in the aftermath of the horrendous Parkland school shooting in 2018, the White House announced that it would meet with representatives of the video game industry to explore a possible causative relationship between virtual violence and realworld violence.

In the court of public opinion, the conclusion of this meeting is a given. Video games are harmful. Yet, the data is less convincing. To pin a violent action on *any* singular cause is dubious and overly simplistic, not to mention impossible to prove. In fact, the rise in the consumption of violent video games since the early 90s has actually been matched by a *decrease* in overall youth violence (perhaps the youth are all inside playing games?). Beneath the surface of knee-jerk reactions and hot takes is a sea of inconclusive studies and mixed data.

At the same time, the notion that spending 12–15 hours per week engaged in *any* activity—all the more one as visceral and addictive as gaming—has *no* effect is equally as absurd. Spending hours on end shooting enemies in a graphic explosion of blood and gore is desensitizing, not to mention almost certainly immoral. Video games may not compel gamers to act out their gaming fantasies in the real world or turn them into monsters, but as with all entertainment choices, the experience is far from neutral.

I should also note that the conversation regarding the influence of gaming is nearly always in the context of *negative* effects. Yet many role-playing games tell well-crafted stories that are able to transport players into beneficial and educational secondary-world experiences in the same way a gripping novel might. The interactive and participatory nature of video games lends itself to cultivating such experiences. It is no coincidence that many of the most imaginative contemporary authors are also enthusiastic gamers. Video games can inspire new and broader ways of looking at the world, evoke rarely felt emotions, and navigate experiences otherwise untouched. The Max Planck Institute for Human Development actually concluded that playing video games such as Nintendo's *Super Mario Bros* **increases** brain matter, memory formation, strategic thinking, and fine motor skills (my 10-year-old self feels so vindicated).

To Play or Not to Play?

Nothing in the Bible unquestionably deems video games inherently sinful. But Christians should prayerfully consider whether or to what degree they should play video games. In the absence of a "thou shalt not play video games" Bible verse, the best guiding principle is Jesus' urging for His followers to be *"as wise as serpents and innocent as doves" (Matt. 10:16).* Here are three guidelines for Christians on this important issue:

1. Make Wise Choices

The fact that there are graphically violent and desensitizing video games does not mean all video games should be off limits, just as the existence of raunchy romance novels shouldn't prevent a Christian from reading a book by Charles Dickens. There are good movies and unwholesome ones, thought-provoking shows and garbage shows, edifying music and demeaning music. No one-size-fits-all mentality can help us navigate entertainment, including video games. Christians should be intentional and aware of the images and virtual stories in which they are immersing themselves. Games that involve vicarious sin and immorality should be avoided. Graphic sexuality and (in most cases) extreme violence should likewise be shunned. Christians are called to be holy, and such gaming experiences hinder rather than promote that calling *(1 Pet. 2:9)*.

2. Maintain Moderation

Arguably, the single most concerning aspect of video games is the time they consume. This issue is not unique to gaming. Any activity performed in excess can be damaging, even Bible reading if one spends day and night studying scripture and leaves no time to *live* and *obey* it. But unlike a movie with a clearly defined time investment, video games often invite prolonged or even indefinite play time. Players can log *hundreds* of hours in a single immersive, open-world game. Video games can be a relaxing pastime in moderation but will severely damage mental, physical, and—most importantly—spiritual health when consumed gluttonously. The apostle Paul wrote, *"'All things are lawful for me,' but not all things are helpful" (1 Cor. 6:12)*. When overindulgent gaming causes us to start neglecting more important and spiritually necessary responsibilities, then we have allowed it too great a foothold in our life.

> As Christians, we have far more important priorities than video games. But if we approach them with wisdom and keep them in their proper place, video games can actually bring people together.

3. Proper Purpose

I am by no means a "gamer," but I enjoy playing games. Throughout our marriage, my wife and I have played casual co-op games as a way to spend time together in the evening, and I have bonded with my kids over games like *The Legend of Zelda* and *Super Mario*. Video games are often thought of as isolating, but I recently attended the wedding of a lovely couple who met through online gaming (she is from America, and he is from Brazil)! The game *Animal Crossing* proved to be a calming tonic for many people during their lonely and stressful coronavirus quarantine. As Christians, we have far more important priorities than video games. But if we approach them with wisdom and keep them in their proper place, video games can actually bring people together.

No one-size-fits-all mentality can help us navigate entertainment, including video games. Christians should be intentional and aware of the images and virtual stories in which they are immersing themselves.

— Daniel Blackaby

3
Safe Spaces: What Franchise Filmmaking Says about our Culture and Christianity

Donte Slocum

"History merely repeats itself. It has all been done before. Nothing under the sun is truly new. What can you point to that is new? How do you know it didn't already exist long ago? We don't remember what happened in those former times. And in future generations, no one will remember what we are doing now."
—Ecclesiastes 1:9–11

With 2019 in our rearview mirror, we can now look forward to a new decade of movies. While *Bad Boys for Life* and *Sonic the Hedgehog* got the new year off to a rousing start, *Dolittle* became 2020's first bomb, and *Birds of Prey* had its wings clipped. Nonetheless, cinephiles can look forward to anticipated films like *A Quiet Place: Part II*, the new James Bond film *No Time to Die*, Marvel's *Black Widow*, another awkwardly named *Fast and Furious* sequel, oh... wait. See what's happening here?

Though we are starting a new decade, it feels like the same cinematic treadmill. Moviegoers are being subjected to rebootuelitis, a serious condition that develops after watching too many reboots, sequels, remakes, and spinoffs. And these films' continued success feeds Hollywood's parasitic tendencies. Like a tick, Hollywood digs underneath audiences' skin, feeding off society's conjoined desires for nostalgia and safety. This yearning for yesteryear has infected every cultural institution, including American Christianity.

Whether Elijah or Aquinas, Paul or Bonhoeffer, ordinary people throughout history have practiced exceptional faith, becoming extraordinary Christians to showcase a dynamic God to a watching world. Nowadays, more effort is put into distilling a formula for faith than sparking interest among Christians to undergo their own adventure. An epidemic of affluenza binds believers and non-believers alike to safe spaces until arriving safely in their graves. To illustrate my point, I will risk excommunication from our editor-in-chief, who will not like what I have to say about this next topic.

When the original *Star Wars* trilogy came out, it was unlike anything ever seen on screen, an amalgamate of high adventure, space samurai, magic, and special effects. Fandom was passed from generation to generation, creating a new congregation of believers. A divisive prequel trilogy tested fans' faith, but the release of *Star Wars: The Force Awakens* rewarded those who didn't become apostates. Though most fans roared with adulation about the magic returning, there were whispers about this film being a souped-up, refurbished version of *A New Hope*, the cinematic equivalent of a paint job. When *The Force Awakens* director J.J Abrams tagged in Rian Johnson for *Star Wars: The Last Jedi*, fans flooded Rotten Tomatoes with pitchfork and torch emojis, because the film felt like a severe detour, causing Disney to tear the third film from original director Colin Trevorrow and return to safety with Abrams. *Star Wars: Rise of Skywalker* polarized everyone, because it was too nostalgic, too safe, too familiar. Despite *Star Wars* starting as something risky but exciting, after three trilogies it was all routine. The new trilogy combined grossed more than $4 billion.

We long for bold blessings, yet any sign of God doing something new is met with suspicion. American Christianity now resembles franchise filmmaking: a safe derivate of daring original stories. We seek to reap fruits of faith through a formula rather than knowing and following a dynamic God. With the 2020s stretching out on time's highway, make this a decade of exploration. There are great new movies intersecting at the cross and culture. ***2 Corinthians 5: 16–17 NLT*** says it best:

> ***"So we have stopped evaluating others from a human point of view. At one time we thought of Christ merely from a human point of view. How differently we know him now! This means that anyone who belongs to Christ has become a new person. The old life is gone; a new life has begun!"***

We long for bold blessings, yet any sign of God doing something new is met with suspicion. American Christianity now resembles franchise filmmaking: a safe derivate of daring original stories. We seek to reap fruits of faith through a formula rather than knowing and following a dynamic God.

— *Donte Slocum*

4

A Fundamentally Christian Work: The Success of "The Lord of the Rings" 66 Years Later

Daniel Blackaby

It may not yet be as impressive as Bilbo Baggins' "eleventy-first" birthday, but *The Fellowship of the Ring*—the first volume in J. R. R. Tolkien's *The Lord of the Rings*—celebrated its 66th birthday last week.

The book's enduring success is mystifying. Tolkien scholar Tom Shippery notes, "It is in fact hard to think of a work [...] written with less concern for commercial considerations than *The Lord of the Rings*." Nevertheless, few books have been more widely read, cherished, or influential. With more than 150 million copies sold, it is one of the bestselling works in history. A poll by Waterstone's bookstore named it the "Book of the Century," and Amazon customers voted it as the "Book of the Millennium." How has such an odd book become so unexpectedly popular and beloved?

There are, of course, many possible reasons for its success. The most immediate explanation is simply that it's a good book. Memorable heroes, big stakes, epic battles, an immersive fictional world—what's not to love? But countless other stories have featured similar elements to far less impressive results.

Consider Peter Jackson's *The Lord of the Rings* movie adaptations, which blew up the box office by earning nearly $3 billion and immense critical acclaim. The final film alone won a staggering 11 Academy

Awards, the most ever earned by a single film. Yet, unlike almost every similar success, it did not expand its genre. *Iron Man* popularized the superhero genre, *Harry Potter* and *Twilight* the YA genre, but more than 17 years after *The Lord of the Rings* trilogy, there have been no successful fantasy films on the big screen. Why?

I believe the reason is that *The Lord of the Rings* is fundamentally a Christian work, reverberating in our souls in a way that few other stories do.

Fundamentally Christian

The Lord of the Rings is not *about* Christianity, nor is it primarily purposed to *teach* Christian theology, values, or truth. Rather, it *is* Christian. In one of his letters, Tolkien wrote,

"The Lord of the Rings is of course a fundamentally religious and Catholic work; unconsciously so at first, but consciously in the revision. That is why I have not put in, or have cut out, practically all references to anything like 'religion', to cults or practices, in the imaginary world. For the religious element is absorbed into the story and the symbolism" (Letter 142).

Perhaps the best way to understand Tolkien's belief is to contrast him with his dear friend C. S. Lewis. Lewis' *The Chronicles of Narnia* is, at its core, Christian theology covered in the appealing cloak of imaginative fiction. The stories point toward and highlight the Christian elements (to "re-image" them, Lewis claimed). In contrast, in *The Lord of the Rings*, Christianity is infused into the very DNA of the story. Rather than illustrating Christian truth, it embodies it.

In my opinion, this difference is a contributing factor to the comparative failure of the *Narnia* film adaptations, which began with promise but quickly fizzled out. Many children love journeying into Narnia, but in large part, only Christian adults continue to dwell there. There is a degree of trickery, a religious bait-and-switch that turns many adults off, because they feel they've been hoodwinked into attending a Sunday school class. The dividing line between adults who love the Narnia stories and those who do not tends to be between those who share the author's faith and those who do not.

The Lord of the Rings has had a vastly different reception. Tolkien's devout Christian faith rarely deters readers who don't share it. Indeed, director Peter Jackson is an atheist. The official Tolkien Society is made up of a vast array of people from radically different faiths and worldviews. Paradoxically, despite being less overtly and outwardly "Christian," *The Lord of the Rings* offers an honest transparency of

Unlike so much contemporary faith-based art, Tolkien's great tale is not successful in spite of its Christianity but because of it. The world, whether they realize it or not, yearns for what Tolkien's inspirational story embodies.

the author's faith that has disarmed even its most militant opponents.

The book allows readers (and later, to a lesser degree, viewers) to experience Christian truth as living reality rather than a mere concept. It emphasizes the Christian virtues of perseverance, faithfulness, self-sacrifice, and mercy; it provides a parable for overcoming evil and temptation. Its ending—a miraculous salvific victory arriving in the darkest moment of defeat and desire (or what Tolkien called the "eucatastrophe")—profoundly echoes the gospel.

The Lord of the Rings is arguably the most re-read book ever written. Like many others, I make frequent pilgrimages to Middle-earth, re-reading the books at the start of every new year, and I find the experience consistently edifying. Unlike so much contemporary faith-based art, Tolkien's great tale is not successful in spite of its Christianity but because of it. The world, whether they realize it or not, yearns for what Tolkien's inspirational story embodies. The good news—indeed, it can rightly be called *The Good News*—is that, unlike the hobbits, elves, and dragons of Middle-earth, the foundational spiritual reality at the heart of the beloved book is no work of imaginative fiction. It is the astonishing truth of Christianity that has beat at the heart of Tolkien's *The Lord of the Rings* for 66 years and will undoubtedly continue to satisfy readers for many more years until the day when we all set sail from the Grey Havens toward the bliss of the Undying Lands.

5
Cinemas, Stadiums and Sanctuaries

Montgomery Loehlein

On Monday, March 16th, my wife and I went to our local Regal Cinema to watch the new movie *Onward*. I was eager to see it, because I love Pixar movies and was concerned the theaters might close soon due to the COVID-19 crisis. Sure enough, by the following afternoon, major theater chains like AMC and Regal announced that they were closing immediately. The cinemas will be dark for a while.

This situation got me thinking about how our culture enjoys communal experiences. Even with the technologies we have at home, we still desire to leave our house to witness events in person. I am an introvert who loves quiet time alone at home, but I still desire shared experiences. Regardless of how nice my 50-inch 4K TV is, I prefer to see films in a large theater with strangers. Even though sports are easier and cheaper to watch on a screen, I still long to sit in the stands and cheer with other fans. No matter how good my stereo is, it can't compare to being at a live concert and feeling the bass in my stomach. Something in us longs to be in a crowd of people enjoying the same thing at the same time.

Unfortunately, we find ourselves in a time when the "crowd" is essentially illegal. There are no theaters, concerts, or sports events to attend. We're stuck at home clicking through our streaming services, looking for something to captivate us. And though we can catch up on some classic movies or shows we've missed, it's not the same as seeing the new James Bond or Wonder Woman flick on opening night. Our microwave popcorn just doesn't smell as good as the $7 bucket you can get at the movie theater. The NBA playoffs should have been starting this month, but instead the sports pundits are arguing about how great Michael Jordan was. TV channels are even replaying old sporting events, but I don't really want to watch the Falcons lose Super Bowl LI again.

So where's the good in all this? We are starving for entertainment and escape, but I think we are hungering for community even more. The fact that sitting on our secluded couches is unsatisfying ought to tell us something about ourselves. ***"It is not good for man to be alone," Genesis 2:18*** says. Yes, this passage is primarily about marriage, but I think there is a broader truth there. Man is not meant to be independent. Regardless of our marital status or family size, we are all meant to live in communion. This truth is evident in Christ's Church. The idea that we are supposed to have a "personal relationship with Jesus" sounds nice, and it is true in a sense. But it's incomplete. We are called into a relationship with Christ, but as He calls us to Himself, we are brought into His family and join millions of brothers and sisters in His Church. There is no such thing as a lone-ranger Christian. Our final heavenly home will not be an isolated country house; it will be in a crowded city ***(Heb. 11, Rev. 21)***.

In addition to cinemas and stadiums, our local church sanctuaries are also closed. We can't gather. We can't sing praises in harmony. We can't eat the Lord's Supper together. Sermons are recorded for video or podcasts. Communing with the saints is restricted at this time. It's sad. But I hope that this current distress helps us not to take our church families for granted. I hope absence really does make our hearts grow fonder. Let's be eager to greet our spiritual siblings with love. Let's long for our pastors' voices preaching into our souls. Let's look with anticipation to when we can come together again and worship our creator and savior.

The hymn "In Christ Alone" says, *"Then bursting forth in glorious day, up from the grave He rose again."* On Easter, we weren't able to sing these words in unison. Our sanctuaries were empty, but so was the tomb.

We are called into a relationship with Christ, but as He calls us to Himself, we are brought into His family and join millions of brothers and sisters in His Church. There is no such thing as a lone-ranger Christian. Our final heavenly home will not be an isolated country house; it will be in a crowded city (Heb. 11, Rev. 21).

— *Montgomery Loehlein*

6

In Defense of Wonder: Cinema and a Longing for Eden

Daniel Blackaby

The opening scene of *Star Wars: A New Hope* is iconic. The camera slowly pans down into starry space as a small spacecraft desperately races away. Suddenly, a massive Imperial destroyer soars into frame in hot pursuit, the size discrepancy between the ships is almost comical. While perfectly establishing the narrative stakes, the scene does something less tangible. In that one moment, no viewer remains earthbound; all are swept away into a world far beyond. I remember the first time my children journeyed with me to a galaxy far, far away. The awe-struck look on their faces can best be described in just one word: **wonder**.

Legendary director Francis Ford Coppola likened the first movie makers to "magicians," and it's easy to see why. There are moments in cinema that awaken a dormant sense of wonder. These moments, difficult to describe, tap into something deep within us at an emotional and even spiritual level.

For more than a decade, James Cameron's *Avatar* held the crown as the highest-grossing movie of all time. Something about the immersive world of Pandora, experienced on a massive screen, captivated audiences. In fact, of the current **60** top-earning movies of all time, only **seven** lack clear fantastical elements. Included in those seven is *Batman* (twice), *Joker*, *James Bond*, and *Fast and Furious* (twice), none of which truly represent the "real world." Of the 60, only *Titanic* can claim a historic foundation (though one filtered through an imaginative Hollywood lens).

Why are audiences repeatedly drawn to cinematic experiences that usher them away from their earthly realities? Perhaps because we were created for wonder.

Sehnsucht

Could it be that these wanderings are not an escape but a return?

Genesis 3:23 is one of the most heartbreaking verses in the Bible: **"So the Lord God banished him from the Garden of Eden to work the ground from which he had been taken."** The Bible doesn't tell us whether Adam or Eve looked back as they departed, but humanity has been yearning for Eden ever since.

Chronicles of Narnia author C. S. Lewis popularized the German word *Sehnsucht* to describe this sensation. The word means "yearning" or "wistful longing." Lewis himself described it as an "inconsolable longing" within the human heart and soul for "we know not what."

> Christians yearn for Eden, but there is no going back to that paradise. Yet, a hope remains for a future paradise and the re-creation of all that was lost (Rev. 22:1–5). Until that wonderful day, Christians must content themselves to dream, yearn, and wonder.

This spiritual yearning is not limited to fantasy. Sublime music and visual art can fill us with the same sense of wonder. Nostalgia—a booming currency in today's culture—is fueled by a stirring within us that things are not as they ought to be and a wistful remembering of "happier times." While nostalgia temporarily alleviates the sense of loss, it never fully satisfies it. What we have lost goes far beyond our own childhood to the infancy of humanity itself. We yearn not for childhood but for Eden.

Unashamed to Wonder

In the opening of Charles Dickens' novel *Hard Times*, the exceedingly practical schoolmaster Mr. Gradgrind declares, "Now, what I want is, Facts. Teach these boys and girls nothing but Facts. Facts alone are wanted in life. Plant nothing else, and root out everything else. You can only form the minds of reasoning animals upon Facts: nothing else will ever be of any service to them."

In innocent childhood we remain in closest proximity to Eden, but with each year we drift further away from the garden. Christians, for so long accused of being wishful dreamers, have largely pushed back with a rigidly rational faith. But what if Christians *are* wishful dreamers? After all, why shouldn't they be? They most clearly recognize the magnitude of what was lost. While unbelievers may convince themselves to be content in an indifferent world of facts and calculations, Christians know that things are not as they once were. We were created for something more, something we once possessed and will one day experience again.

J. R. R. Tolkien described the longing this way: "Why should a man be scorned, if, finding himself in prison, he tries to get out and go home? Or if, when he cannot do so, he thinks and talks about other topics than jailers and prison-walls?" If this world is not our home, then it is unsurprising that we are continually drawn to fantastical stories and moments of escape.

While such experiences can shake us from our "reality"-induced coma and remind us *to* wonder, they will never fully satisfy as the objects of our wonder. It is worth quoting C. S. Lewis here at length (from *The Weight of Glory*):

> The books or the music in which we thought the beauty was located will betray us if we trust to them; it was not in them, it only came through them, and what came through them was longing. These things—the beauty, the memory of our own past—are good images of what we really desire; but if they are mistaken for the thing itself they turn into dumb idols, breaking the hearts of their worshipers. For they are not the thing itself; they are only the scent of a flower we have not found, the echo of a tune we have not heard, news from a country we have never visited.

A prisoner may dream of a long-gone freedom, but the only hope for true freedom lies not behind but ahead. Christians yearn for Eden, but there is no going back to that paradise. Yet, a hope remains for a future paradise and the re-creation of all that was lost *(Rev. 22:1–5)*. Until that wonderful day, Christians must content themselves to dream, yearn, and *wonder*.

7
Should Christians Watch Horror Movies?

Daniel Cabal

How far does Christian liberty extend? Many Christians are reasonably concerned about the horror genre. They may wonder, "Why would my friend who wants to see this horror movie even wish to feel scared?" or "Don't horror movies blaspheme God?"

Some Christians enjoy horror movies but don't discuss them with others, because they lack answers to questions like, "Is it sinful to enjoy a horror movie?"

In this article, I'll establish a few reasons to view horror as "in-bounds" for Christians. But first, let's clear up misunderstandings about the genre.

Horror and Human Emotion

The horror genre contains lots of sub-genres, including monster movies, body horror films, slashers, mysteries, art movies, and more. Each sub-genre corresponds to different filmmakers' attempts to elicit emotions besides fear. A person unfamiliar with horror may be surprised to learn that many movies in the genre emphasize disgust, arousal, and/or sadism rather than fear. A Christian should approach each emotion with a biblically informed outlook.

The Bible does not forbid feeling disgust. Disgust is an appropriate reaction to disgusting things. It is possible that inducing disgust in an audience by portraying harmful acts against human bodies crosses the line into disrespecting God's creation, but believers should remember there is nothing inherently immoral with disgust itself. It's an unpleasant emotion, so most people understandably shun it. But believers should show equal discernment when they encounter entertainment that encourages disgust for God's message of salvation and sin. Feeling disgust at an image of grotesqueness may be more morally appropriate than laughing alongside those who lob quips at Jesus' teachings, for example.

The next emotion associated with the horror genre—and one some movies strive to provoke—is arousal. Arousal in marriage is holy, beautiful, exciting, and beneficial, but outside of marriage it is a dangerous temptation. Jesus spoke clearly (and violently) about the sinfulness of seeking arousal outside of marriage. In **Matthew 5:28–29**, He said, **"Anyone who looks at a woman lustfully has already committed adultery with her in his heart. If your right eye causes you to stumble, gouge it out and throw it away"**. Put bluntly, people who watch horror movies primarily for erotic thrills should repent.

Lastly, sadism is not an emotion per se but rather the experience of feeling pleasure at someone else's physical pain. More than any other horror sub-genre, "slashers" are prone to promoting sadism. But the Bible encourages believers not to **"rejoice when your enemies fall; don't be happy when they stumble" (Prov. 24:17)**. Clearly, enjoying the depiction of another person's suffering should be avoided. And when sadism is present in genres besides horror (such as in action movies when the villain gets his comeuppance), we would do well to eschew it there too!

Your motivation when watching a horror movie (or anything else) certainly matters. Watching a movie with the intention of enjoying vicarious sin is, at best, close to sin itself. But just as Christians can learn to recognize when a conversationalist is likely to steer a discussion toward sin, moviegoers can learn to discern which movies are appropriate for them without abstaining from movies altogether.

Besides scenes intending to evoke sadism, arousal, or disgust, what about when horror movies contain content that deals with death, grief, and fear? Many Christians may avoid the horror genre because they do not want to think about such harsh content. They are entirely within their freedom in Christ to do so. But Christians are not required to avoid a genre due to rough content. While children should be protected from ideas and images they are unable to process, adults have a far greater capacity to know themselves and what they can handle.

Thrills and God-Given Liberty

The best horror movies tell stories in such a way that the audience progresses from a sense of normalcy to discomfort to fear. Again, I am not necessarily trying to explain why people may wish to have this experience. Instead, I want to examine what the Bible says about liberty and fear.

The Bible was written almost two millennia before cinema existed, but it offers us guidance on entertainment choices. The first question we could ask is whether the Bible prohibits feeling afraid. The Bible's response is *only in certain situations in which Christians are encouraged to face their fear*.

The Bible contains numerous accounts of people who were thrown into frightening and overwhelming situations, and in many cases, they were encouraged not to fear because God was (and is!) sovereign. But in other situations, the Bible makes no mention that it was wrong for people to be afraid, perhaps for the same reason it doesn't mention that they needed to eat, sleep, or use the bathroom. Being afraid is a normal response to many situations.

The second question we should ask is if the Bible offers liberty in making choices. Yes, it explicitly affirms that Christians are liberated to enjoy life in God's freedom. Utilizing wisdom in choosing a horror film to watch is then no different than selecting a knife for whittling or lighting a campfire to roast marshmallows—fire and knives are both dangerous when misused, but they are not inherently bad. Many inventions from rollercoasters to sports offer delightful thrills that need no further justification. A liberty that permits others to do only the things one prefers is not a robust liberty at all. The freedom Jesus offers is far stronger. Christians can watch horror movies without apology if they do so wisely.

Furthermore, Christians who are concerned about scares should realize that genres besides horror often contain elements of fear. To be clear, there are aspects of horror in many other movies that range from classic Disney films to *The Wizard of Oz* (1939). Arguing that any movie that makes people feel scared should be off-limits is effectively sweeping countless films off the table. Before banning a considerable number of movies from God's spacious bounds of Christian liberty, one should present a substantially better argument than "I personally dislike it."

Potential Reasons to Watch a Horror Film

You may concede that watching scary movies is not sinful, but you might still feel curious about non-sinful reasons to watch a horror movie. Here are three quick ones!

We know that sad stories offer catharsis, and spicy sauces offer a rush of intensity followed by pleasing relief. In the same way, a scary movie can make viewers experience extreme alertness and then a cooling respite as they return to normalcy. Because people rarely feel endangered by watching a film, exercising the little-used emotion of fear causes it to ache pleasantly.

Second, horror is unique in that it offers pleasures whether it succeeds in being scary or not. Jokes that aren't funny are simply awkward. But it can feel empowering when a scary story is unable to frighten you.

The introduction to *Philosophy of Horror* (2010, edited by Thomas Fahy) offers a defense of horror's societal value. Fahy shows that horror movies' educational significance, quite apart from their capacity to entertain, lies in their ability to remind us that we are not in control. Fahey does not connect this point to a Christian view of God, but believers need not be afraid of horror films or life, knowing that even though they are not in control, God in His love remains sovereign.

Believers need not be afraid of horror films or life, knowing that even though they are not in control, God in His love remains sovereign.

— *Daniel Cabal*

8

JAWS:
An Unexpectedly Timely
Message for the Church

Daniel Blackaby

Steven Spielberg's 1975 blockbuster classic *JAWS* is the greatest movie ever made and perhaps the peak artistic achievement in the history of Western civilization. Okay, that assessment might be a tad hyperbolic. Nevertheless, *JAWS* has long been my favorite film. Due to the misfortune of being born 12 years after it was released, I did not have the opportunity to see it in a movie theater until last week, as movie theaters across the nation have reopened to show classic films. I enjoyed the film as much as I always do, but I was also struck by its timelessness. It has an important message for Christians. No, it is not a neat and tidy C. S. Lewis-esque Christian parable, but *JAWS* offers an inspiring challenge for the Church today.

A Looming Threat and an Unavoidable Crisis

JAWS is a movie about a crisis—a crisis in the form of a 25-foot, man-eating great white shark. What makes the film timeless (and *timely*) is that, much like the whale in Herman Melville's *Moby Dick*, the titular fish is as much a metaphor as it is a sea creature. The antagonistic shark embodies fear and danger; it is the unseen terror lurking at the edge of a peaceful and routine life. The story is primarily about how people respond—for better or worse—when crisis strikes.

Whether we live on the coast or far inland, the Bible reveals that we have a similar terror lurking in our world: ***"The devil prowls around like a roaring lion looking for someone to devour" (1 Pet. 5:8)***. How will we, the Church, confront this threat?

From Dry-Toed to Soaking Wet

In *JAWS*, Martin Brody (Roy Scheider) is the island's new chief of police, having moved from New York. Unlike in the big city, he believes he can make a real difference on the small island, even though he is terrified of the water.

In one of the early shark attack scenes, Brody runs along the beach yelling for the swimmers to get out of the water. He stands on the shore, tiptoeing down the water's edge and never getting his toes wet as he tries to protect the citizens from the approaching danger. I felt convicted that the Church is often like Brody, called to help those in the ocean but unwilling to get wet ourselves; beckoning those lost in the world to come to our safe buildings rather than leaving those sanctuaries and wading into the water to help.

Brody's resolve changes when the shark almost claims his son's life. Spielberg uses a brilliant tracking shot from Brody's POV as he gazes out at the ocean, the movement of the camera symbolizing his newfound understanding that he must enter the ocean and confront the threat.

This moment sets up the satisfying ending, showcasing the character growth from water-fearing outsider to water-soaked hero. In the final showdown, Brody rests on the mast of the ship as it slowly sinks into the ocean and the shark swims straight toward him. The character who once tried to protect people without getting wet is almost fully submerged as he fires his rifle, exploding the air canister caught in the shark's mouth and saving the island.

Unified Diversity

Chief Brody is joined by Matt Hooper (Richard Dreyfuss), a marine biologist and shark expert, and Quint (Robert Shaw), a Captain Ahab-inspired professional shark hunter. After the midpoint of the film, the story focuses exclusively on this trinity of characters as they hunt the man-eating shark. In the process, the thrown-together crew of the *Orca* provides a compelling picture of how the Church should function.

Quint represents the "old school" tradition, while Hooper represents the new. Quint prefers the archaic method of drawing the shark in close and stabbing it with a blade, whereas Hooper brings aboard a wide collection of fancy gear and gadgets. Both men are distrustful of the other, their prejudices leading them to judge and look down on each other. Brody—an inexperienced seaman—is trapped in the middle, a proverbial angel on each shoulder.

There is no forced, sentimental moment when the characters suddenly grasp hands and declare, "I guess we needed each other after all!" Yet, over the course of their shark hunt, they slowly become united. Hooper defers to Quint's hands-on expertise, and Quint is eventually willing to try Hooper's modern methods. Their unity is finally achieved in the film's standout scene.

> There are crises in the world today, and America needs the Church to work together, get into the water, and make a difference. JAWS provides a timely metaphor for the Church; but in the end, it's up to us to live it.

At the start of the scene, all three characters are physically separated from each other, which represents their distrust and disunity. Quint and Hooper begin comparing "scars," attempting to one-up each other. In the process, they move physically and figuratively closer until their legs are overlapped on the table, having found a shared experience and humanity. By the end of the scene (after Robert Shaw's exquisite monologue), all three characters are sitting together at the table singing and laughing, a team at last.

During the final showdown between Brody and the shark, the shark is defeated by a combination of both Quint's and Hooper's methods—Quint's rifle and Hooper's air canister. All three men brought a different area of expertise, experience, and personality to their small crew, and in the end, only by coming together could they overcome the crisis.

The Bible describes the Church as one body with many parts. While we are not submerged in shark-infested waters, we are baptized by one Spirit *(1 Cor. 12:12–13)*. Diverse believers are brought together and unified by a greater purpose. We might be tempted to look down on another part of the body or distrust what is different or unfamiliar. A film like *JAWS*, perhaps unexpectedly, reminds us that we have a greater calling.

There are crises in the world today, and America needs the Church to work together, get into the water, and make a difference. *JAWS* provides a timely metaphor for the Church; but in the end, it's up to us to live it.

9

'The Dark Knight': Twelve Years Later

Montgomery Loehlein

A few days ago, my wife and I went to a movie. Yes, we went to a movie in a physical, brick-and-mortar movie theater. Not many cinemas have reopened yet, and the ones that have aren't showing new releases, just classic films. But I was eager to be in front of the big screen again, and even more eager to revisit one of this century's most influential films: *The Dark Knight*.

The Dark Knight was released July 18, 2008. It was the much-anticipated sequel to Christopher Nolan's reboot of the caped crusader, *Batman Begins*. If we go back in time, we will see that the movie landscape was quite different then. *The Dark Knight* made more than $1 billion in global box office sales, something only five other films had done to that point, and none of them were superhero flicks. Now, if we look at the global records, we'll see that it has moved from 6th to 46th. It slid from highest-grossing comic-book-inspired movie down to 13th highest. The year 2008 saw not only *The Dark Knight* but also Marvel's first entry into the cinematic universe with *Iron Man*. Since these two films were released, superhero movies have dominated ticket sales and essentially become their own film genre. But even with several comic book movies released each year, none, not even *The Avengers*, have captured the same magic as *The Dark Knight*.

Though it has fallen in ticket records, it stays strong in reviews. A 2017 article from *USA Today* ranked it as the 6th greatest film of all time. A 2018 survey from *Empire Magazine* placed it at #3. Currently, it ranks 4th among IMDb's top-rated movies by users.

Why So Spectacular?

So, what is the magic in *The Dark Knight*? Why does it stand out from the myriad of action spectacles we have seen this century? Here are some obvious answers.

First, if you ask people what the best part of the movie is, most will cite Heath Ledger's Oscar-winning performance as the iconic villain Joker. He was humorous yet deeply disturbing. He seemed certifiably insane yet also genius. I could go on, but Ledger's work was undeniably fantastic. There is no argument here.

Second, Cristopher Nolan's direction is grounded and realistic. Gotham City is not some cartoon town from the nineties anymore. It feels like a real American city. This film is a crime drama, not a fantasy. There are so many police, attorney, accountant, and mob boss characters that it's easy to accept one billionaire playboy in a bat suit. The action feels real, and if you watch some behind-the-scenes clips, you'll see that much of it was real. Unlike many directors today, Nolan leans heavily on practical effects, not CGI. So, when you see a semi-truck flip in Gotham City, it looks fantastic, because they literally flipped a semi-truck in downtown Chicago. Nolan's pacing is also vital to the experience. A new shocking event occurs every 15 minutes. Suspense is constant, almost like a horror movie. The clock is always ticking as viewers follow multiple characters and storylines across the city. Yet, even with this tension, Nolan manages to provide moments of quiet contemplation and memorable dialogue scenes.

There are many other excellent aspects of *The Dark Knight* that I could fawn over all day. Its epic score, sharp script, deep supporting cast, and beautiful cinematography are all top notch. But I want to focus on some of its subtleties in storytelling I believe are deeply profound.

"Some men just want to watch the world burn."—Alfred Pennyworth

The Joker loves chaos, because it unsettles powerful people. Those with control and "plans" are left feeling powerless by the Joker's chaotic style of terrorism. Anarchy is the name of the game. He doesn't want money or power. He wants to corrupt all that is good in Gotham. He uses multiple means to accomplish his goal, but his biggest and most terrible achievement isn't a robbery, explosion, or murder; it is turning Harvey Dent.

Bruce Wayne wants Dent to be the savior of Gotham. He thinks that if Dent eradicates organized crime, then the bat suit could be put away. Alas, in two simultaneous explosions, the Joker murders Rachel Dawes, the love interest of both Dent and Wayne, and disfigures Dent's face. Wayne is distraught, but Dent loses his soul. Dent embraces some of the Joker's chaotic methods in his pursuit of revenge against all that wronged him.

The Joker is a scary villain, because he doesn't just want to cause harm; he wants to make others as evil as he is. He is an accuser, or shall I say, devil? He tempts Dent to sin so that Dent will be impure and all of Dent's good deeds will be rendered void.

"At what cost?"—Lucius Fox

Another theme in *The Dark Knight* is the age-old question, "Do the ends justify the means?" Joker is a terrible force that must be stopped. So, Wayne uses his company's technology to spy on every cell phone in the city in order to find him.

Was that action ethical? Maybe. The movie doesn't offer a clear answer. Let's consider our reality for a second. Should the U.S. government spy on its citizens as a means of catching terrorists? You can answer that question for yourself. My point is that grey areas exist. What Batman does is "wrong" to a point, but he acknowledges that it is. What's important is that he doesn't give himself that omniscient power. He trusts it to someone else, Lucius Fox, who recognizes how invasive the tactic is. The technology is used and then immediately destroyed. Fox and Wayne understand the dangers of such power. They don't let it fall into other hands or corrupt their own.

"You either die a hero or live long enough to see yourself become the villain."—Harvey Dent

I'm not sure how you could watch this film and not see Batman as a Christ-type figure. At the end, the Joker is captured, but it seems like he has still won. Dent is not only dead but his reputation is also going to die when news spreads about his murderous last days. I find the dialogue between Gordon and Batman at the end of the movie quite profound:

> *Gordon:* All of Harvey's prosecutions, everything he fought for... undone. Whatever chance you gave us of fixing our city dies with Harvey's reputation. We bet it all on him. The Joker took the best of us and tore him down. People will lose hope.
>
> *Batman:* They won't. They must never know what he did.
>
> *Gordon:* Five dead, two of them cops... you can't sweep that up.
>
> *Batman:* No. But the Joker cannot win... Gotham needs its true hero.
>
> *Gordon:* No!
>
> *Batman:* "You either die a hero, or you live long enough to see yourself become the villain." I can do those things, because

I'm not a hero, not like Dent. I killed those people, that's what I can be.

Gordon: No, you can't! You're not!

Batman: I'm whatever Gotham needs me to be... Call it in.

This scene is a lesson in self-sacrifice. *The Dark Knight* subverts the superhero genre. It's the first Batman movie without Batman in the title. Commissioner Gordon describes him as a knight, but not a shining one. This knight has a suit of armor, a noble steed (the Bat-pod), and a chivalrous code (no guns; no killing), but he stays in the shadows. Rather than pursuing honor, he takes the shame of another man's sins upon himself. He exchanges glory for darkness. He is willing not to be the hero, which is why he is such a great hero.

Rather than pursuing honor, he takes the shame of another man's sins upon himself. He exchanges glory for darkness. He is willing not to be the hero, which is why he is such a great hero.

— *Montgomery Loehlein*

Part Two
WORLDVIEW COLLISIONS

10
Becoming A Christian Culture Changer

Daniel Blackaby

"What has Athens to do with Jerusalem?"

An early theologian named Tertullian asked this question in the 2nd century, and it continues to echo today. At the time, Jerusalem was the center of the religious world, and Athens was the epicenter for culture and the arts. A modern paraphrase might be, "What has Hollywood to do with the Bible Belt?" Or, more broadly, "What does the realm of entertainment and the arts have to do with the Church and the Christian faith?"

For Tertullian—and many Christians since—the answer was *nothing*. A great chasm exists between the two worlds and the wider the better. While the Church must be ever vigilant to avoid Hollywoodization, this aggressively combative posture is not only short-sighted but also unbiblical.

Christians are called to be culture changers, and they cannot accomplish their goal from the outside looking in.

In the World

What did Jesus mean when He commissioned His followers to **"go and make disciples of all nations" (Matt. 28:19)**? One obvious meaning is "to the ends of the earth." But does that interpretation encompass all He meant? A "nation" is far more than a geographical categorization. When we speak of America, we reference more than the landmass sandwiched between Canada and Mexico. We are referring to a mindset, culture, and way of life. We say we are proud to be American not because there is anything special about our soil but because we value freedom and liberty.

When Jesus uttered a commissioning prayer for His disciples, He said to His heavenly Father, *"As you sent me into the world, I have sent them into the world" (John 17:18)*. God the Father sent Jesus to take the Kingdom of God to the very heart of the existing culture. While never sacrificing the truth of His divine nature, Christ willingly recontextualized Himself, leaving the glory of heaven to take human form.

Earlier in that same prayer, Jesus said, *"My prayer is not that you take them out of the world but that you protect them from the evil one" (John 17:15)*. Soldiers don't require protection while on home leave; they need it while serving on the front lines. Jesus never intended for His followers to isolate themselves from the world. In fact, He sent them right into the heart of the culture to be salt and light in places that needed more of both.

Setting the Scene

As Christians, we sometimes think of evangelism in a solely individualistic sense. We spend years fostering a relationship and then we share the gospel and ask for a response. During an age when organized religion is viewed with increased skepticism (if not outright hostility), this method remains a powerful and effective way to communicate our faith.

At the same time, the Church should not turn a blind eye to the influence the larger culture has in framing and directing these evangelistic conversations. Christians have a tendency to be reactionary, standing downstream of culture and waiting for any fish to navigate through the perilous rapids of pop culture before attempting to engage as "fishers of men." But by the time the fish arrive, their minds are already filled with conflicting worldviews and beliefs.

Consider the following:

Last year *Star Wars: The Rise of Skywalker* featured the franchise's first lesbian kiss, and the Marvel Cinematic Universe included its first openly gay character and revealed that Tessa Thompson's Valkyrie will be the first LBGTQ hero in the upcoming film *Thor: Love and Thunder*. Not to miss the boat of the ongoing sexual revolution, the sexual identity of Harry Potter's bearded mentor Dumbledore is slated to continue playing a key role in the upcoming *Fantastic Beasts* sequels. Taylor Swift added to the conversation with her award-winning song "You Need to Calm Down," which paints anyone who upholds a traditional view of marriage as angry, outdated, dim-witted bigots.

> As Christians, we have a role to play in influencing the culture that is shaping both us and the people we are called to reach with the gospel. It is time for the Church to go beyond just condemning or bemoaning the culture and start changing it.

Rapper Eminem surprised the world by unexpectedly dropping his new album *Music to Be Murdered By*, using his first single to take a firm stance on the issue of gun rights. At the Golden Globes, actress Michelle Williams used her acceptance speech to praise the beautiful freedom of having an abortion and was met with cheers and happy tears. Greta Gerwig's adaptation of *Little Women* altered the ending of Alcott's beloved novel for a more feminist portrayal. Star-studded *Bombshell* probed issues of toxic masculinity and the *#MeToo* movement. Controversial *Joker* sparked numerous questions about society, mental health, and authority. The Oscar nominations triggered countless clickbait headlines on racism and sexism. In the athletic realm, superstar NFL quarterback Aaron Rodgers spoke out against religion in a recent podcast.

Shaping the Culture That Shapes Us

These examples contribute to the culture in which we live. As Winston Churchill once said, "We shape our buildings; thereafter they shape us." People are shaped by the world around them. The Church can be vigilant at keeping the world's influence at bay, but it cannot—or at least, *should* not—keep people at bay; and any time Christians relate to people, they come face to face with the influence of the world.

We may not want to keep up with what is happening in pop culture because "it's not really our thing," but let's not forget that the Christian life involves more than just us. For Christians to fulfill their commission, we need to do more than merely exist. If existing as physical beings on this planet was all that mattered, Jesus would not need to *send* us into the world.

As Christians, we have a role to play in influencing the culture that is shaping both us and the people we are called to reach with the gospel. It is time for the Church to go beyond just condemning or bemoaning the culture and start changing it.

11
Irrational Christians for an Irrational World

Daniel Blackaby

We live in an irrational culture.

Postmodernism is largely a myth, an airy talking point university intellectuals bat around but no one truly embraces. As has often been said, not even postmodernism can exist in a postmodern world, as to declare that "there is no objective truth" requires a statement of objective truth. People do not actually believe there is no truth.

At the same time, this "truth" has become further and further removed from any reasonable foundation. Highly educated individuals profess that all religions or spiritual beliefs—despite their contradictory truth claims—will lead to heaven if a person *believes* hard enough. Even scientists, modern culture's self-professed flag bearers of reason, are unfazed by the notion that a human being with male reproductive organs can, in fact, be female. Feeling trumps biology; emotion eclipses logic; desire usurps common sense.

Postmodernism was a fleeting fad, but irrationality seems to be here to stay. The question, then, is how should Christians live in an increasingly irrational world?

Rational Christians

One way many Christians have attempted to counter the irrationality of modern culture is with rationality. In a peculiar role reversal, Christians now stand firm to preserve logical, empirical truths from the emotional wish-fulfillment fantasies of the secular world.

Apologetics has exploded in popularity, believers are becoming invested in science, and a new wave of Christian conservatives now identify themselves as intellectuals, eager to debate anyone who is willing (or unwilling).

As secular culture loses its grip on rationality, Christians appear ready to step up and claim it for themselves.

The Limitation of Reason

Apologetics is an immensely valuable and important discipline. It's also limited. Many aspects of the faith elude human reason. Any attempt to explain the Holy Trinity (i.e. three in one) on rational grounds results in heresy or a resignation to "mystery." Ditto for the hypostatic union of Jesus (i.e. fully God and fully man). A more honest translation of "God's ways are not our ways" is simply, "Yeah, we have no idea."

Intellectually driven Christianity is frequently disappointing. Today's apologists are essentially offering the same arguments that have been around for centuries, just with an updated coat of paint. There are many Christian scientists but few stories of scientists becoming Christians as a result of science. Intellectualism may win debates, but it seldom changes hearts.

Rational secular culture was unimpressed by irrational Christianity, and now irrational secular culture is equally unmoved by rational Christianity. The same wall exists between the two opposing worldviews; the parties have merely switched sides.

Irrational Christians

If rationality is not the answer for Christians living in an irrational culture, then what is? The apostle Peter, writing about Christians living in a godless culture, said,

> *"Live such good lives among the pagans that, though they accuse you of doing wrong, they may see your good deeds and glorify God on the day he visits us [...] For it is God's will that by doing good you should silence the ignorant talk of foolish people."—1 Pet. 2:12, 15*

In other words, don't concern yourself with convincing a foolish world of their folly or vindicating Christian wisdom. Instead, *live* the faith and allow the truth to speak for itself.

It is not Christianity's rationality that astonishes people but its irrationality—the irrationality of turning the other cheek, loving the unlovable, blessing those who curse you, and the preposterous idea that the God of the universe loves sinful humans enough to allow His

It is not Christianity's rationality that astonishes people but its irrationality— the irrationality of turning the other cheek, loving the unlovable, blessing those who curse you, and the preposterous idea that the God of the universe loves sinful humans enough to allow His own Son to die on a cross for them.

own Son to die on a cross for them.

Human rationality is our domain. Unfathomable, illogical, irrational, divine mystery is God's domain. When we resign ourselves to the field of human rationality, we miss the most amazing and exciting realities about our Creator.

Christians should be well-informed about apologetic proofs and the questions skeptics are asking. After all, Peter also wrote, *"Always be prepared to give an answer to everyone who asks you to give the reason for the hope that you have" (1 Pet. 3:15).* At the same time, our ultimate purpose is not to convince unbelievers that Christians are intelligent and rational; it is to help them see that—in an unfathomable and illogical way—God loves them. It sounds crazy, because it *is* crazy. But perhaps our irrational world is ready for craziness.

12
God is Not (Just) Your Best Friend

Daniel Blackaby

Who is God to you?

A frequent Christian response is, "He's my best friend."

Some Christians may not use those exact words, but their behavior suggests that they embrace the sentiment. This perspective is perhaps most evident in the familiar and casual way we pray: "Hey! What's up, God? It's Daniel here again."

The knowledge that we have a best friend who will never leave or forsake us provides hope and comfort amid the disappointments of a fickle world. Yet, despite the solace this outlook provides, it can be dangerous.

Settling for Second Best

With a "best friend" understanding of God, He essentially becomes a better version of what we already have. We have close friends who are a source of encouragement, advice, and companionship. Then we add God into the mix.

God is unquestionably the *highest* point on the friendship spectrum. But our relationship with Him is a difference of degree rather than of kind. God is simply Best Friend 2.0. A problem is that most people are willing to settle for second best. We may not say so, but our actions expose our easily satisfied standards. An A on our final college exam would be ideal, but we're okay to take a B in order to spend less time studying. Our New Year's resolution diet would be most effective if we followed it to the letter, but by February we're okay with adding additional cheat days. We start saying, "My goal was to lose 20 pounds, but I think I'd be fine with 10." We all want the "best," but more often than not, we settle for "good enough." We then take this same attitude into our relationship with God.

We know God can provide the best advice and guidance for our current situation if we commit to spend an hour praying each morning. But it's easier to text our earthly best friend, so we settle for second best. We know scripture provides the answers we seek, but it's easier to skim a self-help blog, so we compromise. We make New Year's commitments to improve our spiritual disciplines, but life gets busy, so we settle for "good enough."

When God is merely Best Friend 2.0, there's always the temptation to settle for Best Friend 1.0.

The Holiness of God

Our relationship with God is not merely a better version of our earthly friendships; it is a different type of relationship altogether. His guidance is not just the highest degree of earthly wisdom; it flows from the realm of divine omniscience. God is not Best Friend 2.0; He is holy, eternal, perfect, and unchanging. He is *God*.

People talk about "wrestling with God" in the same way they might debate a stubborn co-worker or bicker with their spouse about what color to paint the living room. As my grandfather has bluntly said, "Just who do you think you're wrestling with?"

We can take comfort in the knowledge that God is our best friend. But keep in mind that He is not just our best friend. Indeed, He is far more than that.

When we pray, we're not picking up our iPhone to check in with a good buddy ("Hey, man! Sorry it's been a while, but life has been crazy!"); rather, we are entering into the presence of the perfect creator of the universe. In the Bible, such an experience compelled people to rip off their clothes and fall flat on their face in reverence; it caused faces to glow and people to drop dead!

Fear of the Lord

The "God is my best friend" mindset can be incredibly self-serving. Our focus is on how God relates to *us* rather than on how we ought to relate to Him. Like our earthly best friends, God is an add-on, an important one, of course, but someone we can adapt to our schedule nevertheless.

Have we lost sight of God's holiness? Have we settled for gaining another friend rather than radically reorienting ourselves to a holy God?

Perhaps this "best friend" mentality explains why many Christians struggle with the biblical teaching to fear God (a concept used more than 300 times in the Bible). I once heard someone say, "You don't fear spending time with your best friend." Perhaps not. That is, unless your best friend also holds the world in His hands and rules the universe from a heavenly throne.

It's easy to settle for second best when we have similar options available, but we will hold steadfast and desperately onto something unique and irreplaceable. In the end, we can take comfort in the knowledge that God is our best friend. But keep in mind that He is not *just* our best friend. Indeed, He is far more than that.

13
Is Silence Violence?

Montgomery Loehlein

"Don't speak unless spoken to."

Did your parents ever quote this adage when you were a kid and company was coming over for dinner? If so, they probably had a good reason. Children can say a lot of foolish things, and adults often want to have mature and intelligent conversations. I remember watching *Bambi* as a kid and Thumper the bunny saying, "If you can't say something nice, don't say nothing at all." Double negatives aside, these were wise words. Trying not to insult people seems like a good way to stay out of trouble.

Recently, though, society has taken a different approach. After several cases of social injustice went viral, *#SilenceIsViolence* became a popular hashtag. The point is that we all must speak out about said injustices. This idea is partially inspired by Martin Luther King Jr.'s "Letter from Birmingham Jail," in which he said, "We will have to repent in this generation not merely for the hateful words and actions of the bad people but for the appalling silence of the good people." In his context, MLK was right. But like much on social media, the slogan *#SilenceIsViolence* lacks nuance and balance. A balance I think we can find in the Bible.

The Controlled Tongue

"Whoever restrains his words has knowledge, and he who has a cool spirit is a man of understanding. Even a fool who keeps silent is considered wise; when he closes his lips, he is deemed intelligent."—Proverbs 17:27–28

In today's internet age, we have a blowhorn at our fingertips. Social media lets us feel like writers, journalists, theologians, doctors, politicians, or activists, even though most of us aren't any of those

67

things by trade. We have the power of our voice but often forget that with great power comes great responsibility. As wonderful as this communication age seems, it provides numerous new opportunities to sin. Our culture is terribly reactionary. The command in *James 1:19* to be *"quick to hear, slow to speak, slow to anger"* seems to be a joke to the 21st century. A slanderous story is shared quickly. When it is proven false, it is quietly retracted.

In chapter three, James tells us that "not many of you should be teachers," because God judges teachers with a "greater strictness." We shouldn't speak about things we don't understand. Those who are more studied and experienced ought to be trusted to a greater degree than those who talk in ignorance. When we post things quickly and without adequate knowledge, we act as rash fools. It is better to have patience and listen.

Proverbs also says, *"Whoever belittles his neighbor lacks sense, but a man of understanding remains silent" (11:12)*. Speaking does little good when we can't hold back our insults. Tone matters. A good point is immediately sullied by immature language that personally attacks rather than graciously implores.

The Righteous Tongue

"Open your mouth for the mute, for the rights of all who are destitute. Open your mouth, judge righteously, defend the rights of the poor and needy."—Proverbs 31:8–9

Though the tongue can be used for evil, it can also be used for much good. How can we share the gospel without our tongues? How can we praise God without our tongues?

> We ought to use our tongues for the vulnerable and voiceless. The righteous tongue speaks truth in an evil world.

Similarly, we ought to use our tongues (and keyboards) for the vulnerable and voiceless. The righteous tongue speaks truth in an evil world. The Old Testament prophets often serve as an example of this principle. Think of when Nathan confronted King David about his sins in *2 Samuel 12* or the several times Elijah spoke against King Ahab and Queen Jezebel in *1 Kings*.

There is a time for Christians to speak up with clarity and boldness against the sin in the world. We do so broadly when we share the gospel, which says all men have sinned and all should repent and turn to Christ. We may also denounce sins specifically by speaking about select and prevalent evils that exist in our world today. Christians certainly ought to care about people's souls, but we should also care about people's rights and wellbeing. Fighting for justice and the common good is a practical and essential way to love our neighbors. David said, *"The mouth of the righteous utters wisdom, and his tongue speaks justice" (Ps. 37:30).*

The Wise Tongue

> *"The tongue of the wise commends knowledge, but the mouths of fools pour out folly."—Proverbs 15:2*

We must find a happy medium. A tongue that speaks truth kindly and graciously. A tongue that is controlled and reserved. A tongue that is bold, yet humble. A tongue that knows what it does not know. A tongue that doesn't rush to judgement but is willing to speak up for righteousness.

We ought not use our mouths to *"bless our Lord and Father, and with it curse people who are made in the likeness of God" (James 3:9).* Rather, we should *"Let no corrupting talk come out of your mouths, but only such as is good for building up, as fits the occasion, that it may give grace to those who hear" (Eph. 4:29).*

14

To Boycott or Not to Boycott: Living as Christians in Today's *#CancelCulture*

Daniel Blackaby

The gluttonous hunger of cancel culture is never fully satisfied. Like the allure of the guillotine during the bloody French Revolution, our current society is ever on the lookout for more heads to roll. A week rarely goes by without a *#Boycott_____* hashtag trending on social media (fill in the blank with the flavor of the week).

The *#MeToo* movement that began by exposing some of society's most abusive men eventually deteriorated into a witch hunt in which evidence and believable testimony were cast aside in favor of clickbait headlines and a "who's next?" mentality. Unbelievers boycotted Chick-Fil-A for selling homophobic chicken, and Christians later boycotted the fast-food chain for seemingly caving to outside pressure and changing the recipients of its charitable giving. Disney has been boycotted so often it's hard to believe the company continues to do record-setting business. Boycotts have almost become the default posture for Christians living in an increasingly secular world. But is this approach fruitful? Or is there a better way?

To Boycott...?

The reality is that most art is preachy, and people are typically only bothered by it when they disagree with the message. Movies are powerful forces to spread and normalize worldviews; to think "they're just movies" is naïve. Art influences society as significantly as anything else does. Thus, Christians should be aware of what distorted secular and humanistic truths mainstream culture is spreading. One response is to "vote with your wallet." The reasoning is simple. If enough people boycott a movie (or anything else) that contains troubling messages, the movie will fail, and Hollywood will realize that such messages are unprofitable (and nothing speaks louder or clearer to Hollywood than $$$$). There is a time and place for Christians to gather together, pitchforks and torches in hand, and push back with force.

Not to Boycott...?

The problem is that boycotts are almost never effective. Unbelievers "canceled" Chick-fil-A and Christians "canceled" Disney, but both companies are doing better business today than they ever have. Why? One factor is that boycotts typically galvanize the "other side." When unbelievers boycotted Chick-fil-A, countless Christians took a religious pilgrimage to chicken sandwich Mecca. When Christians boycott a movie for pushing a LGBTQ agenda, the "love is love" crowd flocks to see it with increased numbers.

Another factor is that when *everything* is an outrage, *nothing* is an outrage. Most Christians are simply unwilling to withdraw from all aspects of today's culture. When every day brings a new petition to sign, movie to avoid, or celebrity to deride, many Christians simply shrug and wonder, "What's the point?" Calling for boycotts of every small and insignificant thing has diminished the Church's ability to unite in opposition against what's truly dangerous.

Christian Culture vs. Christians in Culture

Boycotts are all good fun until we're the one being boycotted. On the one hand, Christians are up in arms when secular moviemakers and storytellers push secular worldviews. On the other hand, Christians bemoan that secular movie critics don't give fair treatment or attention to preachy faith-based films. Christians will sign an online petition to boycott a TV show for pushing a secular worldview and then participate in door-to-door evangelism or volunteer at a kid's sports camp that teaches more biblical truth than athletic technique. In short, Christians feel that it is our noble and urgent responsibility to expose the world to our beliefs and worldview but are upset when others attempt to do the same.

If Christians believe we are only able to participate in areas of culture that fully align with our religious beliefs, we better start looking for a secluded mountaintop monastery! Christians are not called to force a secular world to look and act Christian; we were sent to be Christians in a secular world. When Christians spend so much time and energy futilely hammering a circular cultural peg into the square hole of the Christian faith, we miss out on other doorways to be salt and light in culture.

When the apostle Paul addressed the Athenians at the Areopagus, he began by quoting from two Greek poems: "In him we live and move and have our being" and "For we are indeed his offspring." In both cases, the "him" in the quotation referenced Zeus. The pagan poems encapsulated a pagan worldview that fundamentally differed from Paul's own beliefs. Rather than boycotting or "canceling" these false and "dangerous" cultural artifacts, Paul used them as a platform to engage in the cultural conversation of his day.

> The goal is not to change the culture but to change the hearts of the people creating the culture and to stand without compromise for the gospel regardless of how violent and tempestuous the cultural flood grows all around us.

Final Thoughts

To be clear, Christians are free to abstain from any aspects of culture we see fit. We are not obligated to sit through a raunchy or highly violent movie for the sake of "cultural engagement" if doing so infringes on our call to holiness or our commitment to our spouse. Christians should have higher standards regarding entertainment than anyone else does. We *should* feel disappointed and frustrated by the ungodly and anti-biblical messages being forced into seemingly every movie or TV show.

The point is simply that Christians will not fix this disturbing trend by isolating ourselves from culture or by trying to force a godless culture to act godly. Rather, we will impact the culture by being present in it and using the messages in today's entertainment as an opportunity to join the cultural conversations and to talk with our children about the important issues. The goal is not to change the culture but to change the hearts of the people creating the culture and to stand without compromise for the gospel regardless of how violent and tempestuous the cultural flood grows all around us.

15

Christians are Weak (and it's Okay if Everybody Knows it)

Daniel Blackaby

> **"Cast all your anxiety on him because he cares for you"**
> **—1 Peter 5:7**

> *"I will not say: do not weep; for not all tears are an evil."*
> —Gandalf, The Return of the King

> *"Jesus loves me this I know,*
> *For the Bible tells me so.*
> *Little ones to Him belong,*
> *They are weak but He is strong."*
> — "Jesus Loves Me"

Those of us who grew up attending Sunday school had that tune instilled in us from an early age.

"Jesus Loves Me" and countless other worship songs demonstrate that the Church is not shy to declare its weakness before God. But as we age, we become more reluctant to admit this vulnerability to other people.

Recent surveys reveal a widespread consensus, particularly among young adults, that the Church is simply not a safe place to ask hard questions or admit doubts. There is a notion, conscious or unconscious, that mature Christians have a perpetual smile glued to their face and declare, without a single worry in the world, "God is good all the time, and all the time, God is good!"

As a result, many Christians hide their struggles for fear of being outed as a failed or weak Christian. We have seemingly forgotten the beautiful truth we learned in that simple children's song that our strength comes from our weakness.

It's okay for Christians not to be okay.

Fearful Bravery

During crises, the internet becomes populated by countless "hot takes" that declare fear demonstrates a lack of spiritual maturity or faith in God and to worry or feel anxious about life's uncertainties is to doubt God's sovereignty and control.

The Bible tells us that we need not fear, because God is with us. It doesn't teach that fear itself is a sin. I love amusement parks and rollercoasters. As a father, I have taken great joy in watching my 5-year-old twin boys take on increasingly larger and scarier rides. They are terrified as they stand in line, and they don't *stop* being terrified until the ride is over and their heart rates finally slow to normal speeds.

After one particularly frightening ride (a mini "Tower of Terror"), one of my boys admitted, "I wasn't brave, Daddy. I was scared."

"Exactly," I said. "You were scared, and you rode the ride anyway. That is bravery."

Feeling scared is not a weakness. If fear and anxiety were not natural and expected emotions, then the Bible wouldn't spend so much time telling us not to be afraid! The biblical declarations are not intended to diminish the reality of fear but to celebrate the promised hope that transcends fear.

Fear is not a sin. Disobedience *as a result* of our fear is a sin. The anticipation of the painful physical and spiritual experience of the cross led Jesus to sweat drops of blood; but His anguish didn't prevent Him from obeying His heavenly Father and dying for the sins of humanity.

We are not faithful because we are fearless. Rather, it is the reality of fear and anxiety that necessitates faith.

Strength in Weakness

When talking to unbelievers, Christians often affirm, "We're not perfect. We're just like you. We mess up too!" But perhaps this remark would be more self-evident if Christians lowered our spiritual superhero masks and showed our weakness and imperfection for all the world to see.

Christians have doubts, feel depressed, are lonely, harbor regrets, struggle with anxiety, and have bad days.

> We are not faithful because we are fearless. Rather, it is the reality of fear and anxiety that necessitates faith.

The fact that God is in control doesn't mean that the Christian journey is never frightening.

The fact that Jesus is Lord doesn't mean we won't experience periods of loneliness or discouragement.

The fact that God loves us doesn't mean Christians never need a counselor or therapy session.

Perhaps one reason the Church has been a step or two behind the wider culture regarding the importance of mental health is that we've inadvertently bought into the lie that mental illness signals spiritual weakness. We mistakenly assume faith requires the absence of fear and doubt rather than obedience *despite* our fear and doubt.

Christians don't enter into God's presence because we have it all together. Rather, we humbly fall on our face before Jesus because we're *not* strong. The world is a harsh place, and we are desperate for God's supernatural comfort and peace.

Let's not forget that the same Jesus who promised His joy would be made full in us also wept bitter tears and sweat drops of blood. God doesn't promise that we'll never struggle, and He's not fooled by our fake smiles, forced peppiness, and artificial strength. What He *does* promise us is something far greater—that He will never leave us or forsake us, no matter how many times we fail or how difficult this life becomes. Let's use whatever strength we have—weak as we may be—and cling to that hope. Indeed, we are weak, but He is strong.

16
When Christian Leaders Fail

Daniel Blackaby

I recently read Charles Dickens' *A Tale of Two Cities*. Set during the bloody French Revolution, Dickens writes, "La Guillotine... was the sign of the regeneration of the human race. It superseded the Cross. Models of it were worn on breasts from which the Cross was discarded, and it was bowed down to and believed in where the Cross was denied." The guillotine has been retired as an instrument of death, but the same bloodthirst has persisted into the 21st century.

When public figures fail, social media vultures are eager to sink their teeth into the fresh carcass. In the early stages of the *#MeToo* movement, Christian leaders were ousted in bulk portions (including several that hit close to home for me). In the days since, the vultures' feast has settled into a steady diet. Seemingly every month or two another Christian leader is toppled for words or actions that are contrary to Christ-like behavior. Tragically, this cycle has become so common that I fear many Christians have become desensitized to the wreckage left in the wake of these failures.

Does it Matter?

When a notable Christian leader's moral failure becomes public, the response is often a variation of the sentiment, "If the failure of people causes you to drift away from God, then your faith was in people and not in God." Indeed, God is equally as sovereign and holy when His self-proclaimed followers fail as when they are faithful. At the same time, this response is unintentionally selfish and self-serving.

First, it is inevitably given by people of strong faith. It may be true that "If your faith is deterred by human action, then it's a weak faith," but the proper response in such a situation is not simply to cast aside those of weak faith *(Rom. 14:1–23)*.

Second, there is a tendency to adapt the rules on the fly. As the Church, we repeatedly hammer on the importance of representing Christ well. We are lights in the dark world, ambassadors of Christ who reflect the image of Jesus for all to see. When we fall short, however, there is a collective shrug. "Well, it's not about us anyway." The way we represent Jesus to the world is vital and praiseworthy when we succeed but trivial or indifferent when we don't. All the praise, but none of the blame. There is a reason the Bible asserts that teachers are to be judged more strictly than others *(James 3:1)*. Those who represent Christ in a public leadership capacity have immense potential for both good and evil.

The Consequences

Younger Christians are abandoning the Church at alarming rates. There has long been a narrative that when these young Christians graduate from high school, they are simply ill-prepared and thus blindsided by outspoken atheist college professors. But this explanation again seems to shift the responsibility away from the Church (at least in part) and place it on "the world."

> The moral failure and hypocrisy of those within the Church is far more devastating to the faith of the younger generations than are any philosophical arguments by atheists outside of it.

What's lost in this commonly assumed narrative is that the high casualty rate of young believers also exists among those attending private Christian universities where (presumably) no atheist professors are present. Also, the Church "dropouts" themselves rarely give this "big bad college professor" narrative as a major reason they abandoned Christianity. According to LifeWay's most recent research, the primary causes have to do with the actions or failures of those **within the Church**.

In other words, it is not only that an unbelieving world is pulling young Christians away from the Church; it's that the actions of the Church are repelling them or causing them to question what they've been taught. The moral failure and hypocrisy of those within the Church is far more devastating to the faith of the younger generations than are any philosophical arguments by atheists outside of it. The failure of Christian leaders may not hinder Christians of strong faith, but it does impact, often in profound ways, those with a less stable faith.

What Can Be Done?

Hypocrisy in the Church has been around for as long as the Church itself. The apostle Paul was speaking to this same issue 2,000 years ago. What has changed, however, is that social media can now broadcast these failures to a wider audience. Whereas past Christians may have been let down by a local Christian leader or mentor, now such failures become national news. Christian leaders will continue to fail, and the way we approach these failures makes a difference. Here are five ways Christians should respond when their leaders fail:

Examine ourselves. Don't allow our words or actions to give anyone cause to question the God we serve.

Have honest conversations. Don't dismiss another person's disillusionment by saying, "If your faith in God was as strong as ours, then the sinful deeds of man wouldn't impact you!" Rather, walk with people and guide them to that level of faith.

Hold leaders accountable. All Christians should be held accountable, but the unique position of leaders amplifies their influence on the wider culture's view of Christianity.

Call the failures sin, not exceptions. Let's not be too hasty to declare, "They weren't true Christians." Excluding anyone who fails may outwardly seem to safeguard the Church's image, but the younger generations are not impressed by PR gymnastics. Sinful human nature is the rule, not the exception. When Christians sin, let's rightly call it sin.

Pray for those in leadership. Christian leaders may fail, but that should not stop us from praying for them. Let's not be quick to condemn but slow to pray, quick to pull down but slow to build up.

Part Three

MOVIE REVIEWS

17
Mulan (2020)

Carrie Camp

A soulless remake that takes itself way too seriously.

About the Film

A live-action remake of the 1998 animated classic, *Mulan* (2020) tells the story of a young Chinese woman who disguises herself as a man and goes to battle in her aging father's place, ultimately bringing honor to her family and her nation.

Whereas the animated version was heavy on slapstick humor and comic relief (including Eddie Murphy's memorable performance as the voice of the demoted ancestral guardian Mushu), the live-action adaptation pares down the fluff (read: fun and joy) and takes a less lighthearted approach.

With each of the recent live-action remakes, Disney has taken a risk by messing with the arguably untouchable classics. As a mega-fan of the animated version, I found this adaptation to be a much-too-serious action flick stripped of everything that made the animated version great. The fun sidekicks are replaced with a silent phoenix, a visually appealing but ultimately uninteresting metaphor for Mulan's awakening as an empowered woman. The songs show up only in the score as subtle nods to the animated classic. And Mulan's lovable klutziness? Replaced by a fierce warrior who would make the most ferocious Hun quiver in his boots.

What the film has in abundance is battle sequences—and Mulan is right in the thick of them. Rather than a clumsy village girl who achieves success through bravery and clever determination, the Mulan of the live-action remake is essentially a chi-powered Marvel superhero. And she's unstoppable.

For Consideration

On the Surface

Profanity: None.

Sexuality: There are a few scenes of skinny-dipping, though nothing immodest is shown. There are also a few light-hearted scenes of soldiers rolling over in their sleep and unconsciously draping their arms over Mulan (and each other).

Violence: The entire film is essentially an action sequence, though there is very little blood or gore. Some of the scenes might be disturbing for young or sensitive viewers.

Beneath the Surface

Spirituality and the Power of Chi

A common theme throughout the film is the power of chi, a spiritual energy force that flows through exceptional Chinese warriors (in much the same way Jedis draw their strength from the Force). Though the film is somewhat ambiguous regarding the nuances of chi, Mulan is clearly gifted with its power, something that is unacceptable for women in her culture.

Obviously, the supernatural elements portrayed in the film—and there are quite a few—are rooted in the story's historical and mythological context and are incompatible with biblical teachings. Bear that in mind when determining whether to watch the film (or whether to allow your children to watch it).

Female Empowerment

Mulan has always been a symbol of female empowerment. She breaks down the narrow boundaries of what is expected of women in her culture (wife, mother, homemaker) and becomes a kick-butt warrior instead. But in contrast to the 1998 animated version, the live-action Mulan's story is not so much about transformation as it is about embracing the warrior that is already inside her. Her skills stem from a supernatural gift rather than from anything she has worked to achieve (unlike the clumsy-but-clever animated Mulan who attains military victory through grit and quick thinking). While watching Mulan best warriors twice her size in hand-to-hand combat might be enjoyable, it's not particularly relatable (or empowering) for the average chi-less female viewer.

The Importance of Family Honor

Another major theme in the film is the importance of honoring one's family. Mulan must strike a delicate balance between respecting her parents and staying true to who she is. In the end, she finds a way to do both.

Final Verdict

Mulan (2020) is a serious adaptation geared toward a more mature audience. But in shedding the goofy sidekicks, songs, and (most of) Mulan's blunders, the movie loses the charm that made the animated version so much fun to watch. What remains is a Mushu-less action flick that lacks depth, character development, and humor. While fans of *Crouching Tiger Hidden Dragon*-esque films may appreciate the martial arts battle sequences, fans of the original will likely be disappointed.

18
Tenet

Daniel Blackaby

A time-bending thriller that's a little too clever for its own good.

About the Film

Movie theaters have started to open up, and there's arguably no filmmaker better suited to usher audiences back than "Mr. Movie Theater Experience" himself—Christopher Nolan, one of the few working directors who can sell a movie on reputation alone. Nolan's latest blockbuster *Tenet* is perhaps his most Nolan-esque film yet. Whether that description is a ringing endorsement or not will probably depend on how much you enjoy his past works and storytelling sensibilities.

I won't offer a plot summary here. I want to avoid spoilers, but mostly I'm not sure that I could explain this film even if I tried. The complexity of *Tenet* makes his earlier movie *Inception* seem like something that debuted on Nickelodeon Kids. Whereas *Inception* was akin to juggling (with Nolan tossing in one ball after another after another), *Tenet* is more like a puzzle (put together without any discernable order and with a final picture that is difficult to decipher even after completion). The first third of the narrative is almost impossible to follow not only because of the complex time-inversion concept but also because the film does not provide viewers with enough information to understand the events. As the story unfolds and additional exposition is provided, these earlier scenes begin to make more sense. But the film asks viewers to buy in from the start and trust that Nolan is leading to a satisfying payoff.

Nolan has always been a high-concept storyteller. He typically begins with some gimmick or story mechanic (dreams within dreams, alternative dimensions, non-linear storytelling, etc.) and then builds his movies around that singular core concept. The concept, not the characters, drives the stories. In *Tenet*, the protagonist is never even given a name beyond "The Protagonist." Robert Pattinson's character is a standout in every scene but given no backstory or clear motivations.

Sweeping Hollywood romance and a classic hero's journey are pushed to the fringe to make room for some truly impressive scenes utilizing the "time-inversion" concept to dazzling effect. In one such scene showcasing Nolan's quintessential brilliance, two characters fight in a hallway while one is traveling forward in time and the other is traveling backward. In an earlier expositional scene, a character urges John David Washington's lead character, "Don't think it. *Feel* it." This advice works on a meta-level as well. While the film invites (even *demands*) viewers to pay close attention and keep their brains on overdrive, in the end it is a work of entertainment, and its enjoyment comes not in nitpicking or over-analyzing the inevitable paradoxes and inconsistencies of time travel but in appreciating what and how far a filmmaker as capable as Nolan can push those concepts.

For Consideration

On the Surface

Profanity: 1 F-word, various minor profanities and crude references, and several usages of the Lord's name in vain.

Sexuality: None.

Violence: Standard action flick violence. People are shot and die in explosions, but minimal blood or graphic depictions.

Beneath the Surface

The Future against the Past

Without venturing into spoiler territory, one of the underlying themes in *Tenet* is the relationship between the past and the future (the word "Tenet" itself is a palindrome, read the same both forward and backward). More specifically, the film explores the idea that future salvation comes from righting (or erasing) past sins. This concept, while never front and center in the film, is nevertheless an important and timely one. Intentionally or not, *Tenet* arrives in theaters at a time when America is having similar discussions. For many people, the fight for future liberty and justice is achievable only by attempting to correct the failures of the past. Textbooks are rewritten, monuments are pulled down, and long-dead historical figures' closets are checked for skeletons.

The film is not preachy on this point and arguably sends mixed messages. More than once, characters proclaim, "What happened has happened." The past is the past; it can't be changed. Characters journey backward in time to change events only to realize that their presence was always a part of those events. Changing the past, then, comes not in erasing it but from learning from it and moving on.

Faith and Reality

A signature of Christopher Nolan is his ability to follow a scientific concept to its inevitable spiritual conclusion. Although built upon Hollywood-ized science, many of his films ultimately end with a spiritual realization that there is more to reality than we see or realize. *Tenet* is no exception. Near the end of the film, two characters discuss the new non-linear understanding of the world. One of the characters remarks, "Some people call it faith. I call it reality." In other words, the unseen dimension of life is not something that exists apart from or beyond reality but is built into the very nature of reality, whether we have faith in it or not.

Final Verdict

It is rare that a Hollywood blockbuster requires much more thought than getting popcorn from the bag to the mouth. It is a credit to Christopher Nolan's talent that he consistently offers up one fresh and thought-provoking film after another. A movie such as *Tenet* almost necessitates multiple viewings in order to appreciate fully or give an informed evaluation of it. Is it a great movie that is destined to become a classic like *Inception*? I honestly don't know. What I do know is that the film showcases a generational filmmaker pushing his storytelling ability to its extreme edge. That alone makes *Tenet* worth checking out. Just don't expect to understand everything you see!

19

A Beautiful Day in the Neighborhood

Sarah Blackaby

An introspective look at how we interact with people in our lives.

About the Film

This movie caught me off guard. I knew it had been nominated for several awards and had received good word-of-mouth feedback, but I did not expect it to move me as much as it did. The movie is about a character named Lloyd who has been struggling in his relationship with his father. Lloyd is a magazine writer who is assigned to write a piece on Mr. Rogers. Lloyd has a bad reputation for how he portrays people in his stories. He goes into the interview with Mr. Rogers with a certain preconceived idea but ultimately leaves with an impression he can't shake. The movie shows the beautiful compassion Fred Rogers had for humankind. The two main characters build an unlikely friendship as Mr. Rogers helps Lloyd face the anger he's been holding onto, confront the broken relationship with his father, and finally move forward in his life.

For Consideration

On the Surface

Profanity: A couple mild profanities ("d—," "What the h—," "crap").

Sexuality: Marital kissing and cuddling and mild discussions of a man "sleeping around."

Violence: Lloyd and his father get in a fight early on and Lloyd breaks his nose.

There is also some alcohol and substance abuse.

Beneath the Surface

Death of a Loved One

Lloyd's mother is diagnosed with cancer when he is young. When his father leaves them, Lloyd and his sister are left to deal with their ailing mother as she loses her battle with cancer. The movie doesn't show the family going through this struggle on screen, but viewers can piece it together as the movie progresses. This tragedy is the root of the relational issues between Lloyd and his father. The film includes a dream scene between Lloyd and his mother while she is in the hospital that, although a little strange, is a pivotal moment that showcases the pain Lloyd has been feeling. Death is a reality of life. The movie demonstrates that it is okay and healthy to grieve the loss of a loved one. But if we get stuck in our grief, it will hinder every part of our lives.

How to Deal with Anger

Mr. Rogers teaches Lloyd how to deal with his anger toward his father in a healthy way. Anger is a real and justified emotion, but the way we deal with that anger is important. Mr. Rogers teaches alternative methods of releasing anger instead of harming oneself or others. Lloyd struggles to deal with his anger towards his father and has become a bitter and angry man. Mr. Rogers encourages him to forgive his father, and by doing so, he is able to heal and move past his anger.

The Power of Love, Kindness, and Connecting with People

Mr. Rogers is known for his remarkable kindness and love for people. At first this portrayal came across as somewhat awkward. But then I realized the reason it seemed strange was simply because most people aren't that genuinely nice! Tom Hanks does an amazing job of portraying Fred Rogers. Mr. Rogers truly was a beautiful person who took the time to invest in everyone he encountered. My favorite moment in the movie is a scene in which Lloyd and Mr. Rogers are sitting in a Chinese restaurant. Mr. Rogers has Lloyd reflect on all the people who have ever loved him. This request is followed by a long moment of silence during which Tom Hanks looks at the camera. I found myself reflecting on my own life, and it was a wonderful shift in perspective. We often find ourselves dwelling on the negative. Life isn't always perfect, and our circumstances aren't always great. But when we shift our perspective as Mr. Rogers teaches, we can find joy and positivity in the middle of even the most difficult times.

Parents' Influence on Their Children

The dynamic between Lloyd and his wife was interesting to watch. They are new parents, and the movie depicts a lot of the normal "new-parent" struggles. Throughout the film, the viewer sees how Lloyd evolves in his relationship with his son as he lets go of his anger toward his own father. People who have had a strained relationship with their parents often want to do better for their own children, and Lloyd shares that desire. He recognizes that he wants things to be different in his marriage and in his relationship with his son than he experienced as a child. Mr. Rogers talks about how his relationship with his children wasn't perfect but that they came through. It's an encouraging reminder that every parent is going to mess up, and that is okay. It's also a challenging reminder of the immense responsibility that comes with parenthood and how our attitudes—for better or worse—can impact those around us.

Final Verdict

I enjoyed how much this movie made me think about my own life. I thought I was sitting down to watch a movie about Mr. Rogers, but it ended up being more about a man named Lloyd Vogel. It was a beautiful story about how true friendship can change a person's life. I was reminded of the importance of sincerely listening to people. The movie convicted me about what it means to forgive someone and let go of anger. We don't always realize the anger we are holding onto and the power it can have over us. This movie was introspective, and I am glad I watched it.

20
Just Mercy

Donte Slocum

A well-made exploration of power's ability to distort truth.

"The appearance of the law must be upheld, especially when it's being broken." —William "Boss" Tweed, Gangs of New York

About the Film

Throughout America's past and present, minorities have frequently received the brunt of our justice system's injustices. Throughout America's history, the law has been used to protect those in power. White men in positions of power have thrown away generations of black men under false accusations masquerading as justice.

This history of injustice is the historical backdrop of *Just Mercy*. Based on a true story and adapted from a bestselling book, the film follows attorney Bryan Stevenson (Michael B. Jordan). A recent Harvard law school graduate, Stevenson moves to Monroeville, Alabama, to take a job as director of the Equal Justice Initiative. His mission: providing prisoners on death row the quality legal representation they were denied. While researching the case of death row inmate Walter "Johnny D" McMillian (Jamie Foxx), he finds compelling evidence of McMillian's innocence.

For Consideration

On The Surface

<u>Profanity:</u> There is some coarse language, including racial slurs.

Sexuality: None.

Violence: Hinted at but never shown. There is a short scene showing a prisoner's execution by electric chair.

||||||||||||||||||||||||||||||||||||||||||||||||||||||||||||||||||||||||||||||||||||||||||||||||||||||||||||||||||||||||||||||||||||||||||||||||||||||||||||||||||||||||||||||||||

Beneath The Surface

Willful Disinformation

This movie says a lot about our society's tendency to label emotional opinion as rational truth. Walter's conviction was built on flimsy testimony from a convicted white murderer named Ralph Myers (Tim Nelson Blake). Myers never met or saw Walter before testifying against him. Walter was arraigned despite being surrounded by numerous family members and friends at his home during the time of the crime. Not only is Walter sent to death row **before** his trial but none of his family or friends are called as witnesses, and evidence proving his innocence is buried. To top off this disgusting sundae, the presiding judge overturns his original sentence of life in prison, converting his conviction into a death sentence. It's like 2+2=5.

Literature fans should recognize Monroeville, Alabama, as Harper Lee's hometown and her inspiration for *To Kill a Mockingbird*. This fact isn't ignored: District Attorney Tommy Chapman (Rafe Spall) mentions this fun tidbit to Bryan Stevenson without irony.

Just Mercy showcases how destructive lies are when wielded by those in power. During a conversation with Bryan, Walter even admits to doubting his own innocence. Walter McMillian is sentenced to die not based on the criminality of his character but on the color of his skin. For a shattered town seeking sense from a young girl's murder, law enforcement was willing to offer Walter's life to coalesce communal healing. For pursuing truth, Bryan is threatened by those in power, with police officers pointing guns during a "routine" traffic stop and an ordinary citizen calling in a bomb threat at his home. For seeking to balance the scales of justice, Bryan is labeled lawless. For those in law enforcement, white feelings outweigh black innocence.

Mercy for the Convicted

On the flip side, the film also shows guilty prisoners. Herbert Richardson (Rob Morgan) was a mentally troubled Vietnam war veteran convicted of murdering his girlfriend and sentenced to death row. Herbert knows what he's done and believes he deserves to die. After finding out about his past struggles with mental disorders like PTSD, Bryan seeks a stay on Herbert's execution from the Supreme Court. Though his effort fails, Bryan's willingness to help touches Herbert. This type of kindness isn't reserved for the convicted. Their relationship is a beautiful illustration of grace and mercy.

This willingness to humanize prisoners separates *Just Mercy* from more standard-issued court dramas. In a flashback, Bryan connects with a death row inmate over growing up in church. Herbert shares a rapport with fellow death row inmates Walter and Anthony Ray Minton (another wrongful conviction). During Herbert's execution, the remaining death row inmates bang on their cells in unison to show him support. Herbert arranges for music to play during his execution to avoid subjecting his fellow inmates to the noise from the electric chair. These moments provide glimpses of community, even surprising humor. It's a reminder of how even those condemned can display compassion.

Final Verdict

Just Mercy is one of the best films of 2019. Though not a faith-based film, this film's presentation of Christian themes resonates stronger and clearer than even some faith-based movies. Believers should go see this movie. It epitomizes how God can take our most painful moments and use them as a roadmap to help those who suffer injustice and display mercy toward those neglected or undeserving. We are more than the worst things we have done.

Writers

Daniel Blackaby

Daniel is a lifelong lover of culture and the creative arts. He earned a PhD in "Christianity and the Arts" and a ThM in "Philosophy, Worldview, and Apologetics" from the Southern Baptist Theological Seminary, an MDiv from Gateway Seminary, and a BA in English from North Greenville University. He has published multiple books of both fiction and nonfiction, including the YA fantasy trilogy The Lost City Chronicles. He started The Collision in 2019 to equip Christians to engage with and contribute to culture. Daniel is a voracious reader of classic literature, a J. R. R. Tolkien buff, and a connoisseur of European heavy metal. He lives in Georgia with his wife, Sarah, twin boys, Emerson and Logan, and dog named Bilbo.

Montgomery Loehlein

Monty was homeschooled throughout his childhood and values self-education. As a teen, he started reading about theology. What started with a couple of C.S. Lewis books has grown into a great interest in theology. He loves film, particularly old classics and science fiction. Other interests include sports, politics, and lots of podcasts. He currently works for an electrical distributor. Monty also enjoys serving his church in various ways as a deacon. He lives in Georgia with his wife, Shelby, and dog, Martha.

Donte Slocum

Donte is a scriptwriter and cinephile. He graduated with a BA in Telecommunication Arts from the University of Georgia. He has written on a wide array of topics from sports to film. When he is not writing, Donte enjoys watching movies and participating in other nerdy activities.

Sarah Blackaby

Sarah is an artist and teacher. She studied art at the Alberta University of the Arts and earned a certificate in fashion design and marketing from LaSalle College in Vancouver, Canada. Her art has been featured in a wide range of settings, including on multiple book covers and in several illustrated children's books. Sarah hosts painting classes at her home studio and teaches middle school art as a means of training and inspiring the next generation of creative artists. She lives in Jonesboro, GA, with her husband and twin boys, Emerson and Logan.

Carrie Camp

Carrie's writing has been featured in an assortment of literary journals and news outlets. She holds an MFA from Converse College, a Master of Theological Studies degree from Southwestern Baptist Theological Seminary, and a BA from North Greenville University. When she's not writing, she enjoys reading classic literature, traveling, and watching obscure British period dramas. She lives on a small homestead in Georgia with her husband, two daughters, and an ever-expanding menagerie of livestock.

Daniel Cabal

Daniel is a filmmaker, a cinema buff, and a student of the arts. He holds a PhD in "Christianity and the Arts" with a focus on film from the Southern Baptist Theological Seminary and an MDiv from Southwestern Baptist Theological Seminary. He has been a television director for Prestonwood Baptist Church in Dallas, a client manager for IBM, a pastor, a film director, and a humanitarian aid manager and teacher in Afghanistan. He currently lives in Louisville, KY, with his family.

www.ingramcontent.com/pod-product-compliance
Lightning Source LLC
Chambersburg PA
CBHW060952040426
42445CB00011B/1126